I Live Therefore I Write

Alexandra Bailey Coleman

A catalogue record for this work is available from the National Library of Australia

Bailey Coleman, Alexandra (author)
I Live Therefore I Write
ISBN 978-1-922803-18-4
Poetry

Garamond Regular 11/16
Cover and book design by

Green Hill Publishing

For my father -

For reading me Harry Potter as a baby until I drifted off to sleep,
then watching the movies religiously together as I grew older. You took me
on countless adventures in the Big Red Car that I will never forget. Thank
you for introducing me to the world of books, magic and adventure.

For my mother -

I wait for the day when we sit down together and you tell me more of your
stories, sharing with me the magic you have felt and seen in your life. You
have brought so much joy and laughter into my life through the form of
music, movies and jokes. Thank you for your undying love and support.

And for the faceless, nameless people in this novel -

You have faces and names and our love and friendships
live on in these pages. Thank you for teaching me how to
love, how to find myself, and how to write again.

The Loving

You feel it, don't you?
deep within your soul
your belly feeling
like a crumpled car

butterflies the size of birds
the tightness in your chest
and the undeniable smile
that spreads across your face

when you think about him
it's okay to feel vulnerable
that your heart is in his hands
praying he won't crush it

trust the process
trust your gut
trust the good things that
make you feel this way
in the first place

You were the first person
to make me tremble
and quiver from the ways
you moved and touched me

as we caressed each other
and learnt the secrets
of each other's bodies
tucked away in our bedrooms

you deciphered the codes
my body laid out in front of you
and unlocked sensations
I'd never felt before

would our love be forbidden
if we dared to create
art with our bodies
crashing against one another
the shades of our skin melting
into each other?

You were an artist with your love
and my body was your canvas
your hands slid down my skin
and you painted me
the room was silent but
our movements were bursting with
noise and dripping with colour
our lips clashed and I was
splattered, smeared, spotted
with ink and a spectrum
my back was painted peach
and purples and rose
my legs were scarlet and marigold
my neck was coated in seafoam and
indigo as your tangerine lips left
their watermark across my body
my face splashed with gold and
bronze and ambers
your love turned me into
a peacock on display
you stared at your work in wonder
and before the light faded in the
workshop we created in your
bedroom you whispered to me:

'mesmerising'

You coloured my monochrome life

with highlighter

'neon'

Your eyes were deeper
than underwater caverns
and richer than the
darkest chocolate.
coated with honey
your skin glistened
as if the sun only
shines for you.
your lips enveloped me
like a warm embrace
I fell into your kiss
every time

The golden hue of his skin
the ebony curls
the thick brushy eyebrows and
the mile-long eyelashes

'details I'

I crave you
like an addict
craves another hit
when you aren't around
I'll need a distraction
to keep you off my mind

I want you
not like a child
wants a toy or a lolly
but with passion, desire, lust,
for our bodies to collide
and move together as one

Every moment I see you
when I blink you are burnt
into my eyesockets

I want you to collide with me
in the midnight hour
when the moon rises into the sky
acting like a spotlight to our stage
as we debut in our love affair

My body is like a barren wasteland
begging for you to return like
long-awaited rain to replenish me

'barren'

Alex Bailey Coleman

The sunlight creeps in
the dust flies peacefully
around your room
glimmering in the soft
morning light
your skin is illuminated
your hair like starlight
in the stream of sunlight
that sneaks through the curtains
the curls are unruly and untameable
and your eyes are deep and rich
and glazed over as you
still make your way out of
your half-asleep state

'a memory'

When I first met him
I knew somewhere
secretly
in my heart
that he would be
the best and
the worst thing
that would ever happen
to me

when I first met him
I knew
that I loved him;
when he smiled at me
when he hugged me
when he looked at me
the way only he can,

I had no idea
after so long
since we first met
that he would still lurk
in my thoughts

I had no idea
he could still
leave me breathless
when he smiles at me
I had no idea
he could still
twist my stomach into knots
when he looks at me.
in the years we've known
each other
I am still surprised
by how hard I
fall
for you every goddamn time
you smile like
that

I wish you understood
what goes through my mind
when you talk
when you laugh
when you look at me
the way only you can

'can you hear'

I wish you understood
what my heart does to me
when I talk back
when I laugh
when I look at you
just a second too long

'my heart racing?'

When you are around me
I see everything else fade away
and instead everything floods my open eyes
pouring in with a new, wonderful light.

How is it
that I feel like I'm
floating on thin air
higher than cloud nine
when I'm with you

but feel so cold and fragile
like prized crystal
so ready to shatter
without you?

'the high is just as wild as the low'

Can only love
hurt like
this?
or is it
obsession
careening through
my veins
when my heart
jolts like a
car crash
against my
ribs
and my brain,
infected with a
lovesick virus,
replays the image
of you
in my head?

I wanted to freeze every moment from this morning. you were still half asleep, with your head nuzzled into my shoulder, your long arms curled around my body, strong and safe. the warmth of our bodies lying together cut by the crisp morning – the sun hadn't quite risen over the tall terrace houses around us. your soft breath warm and sweet against my neck, the occasional grumble escaping your throat reminded me of a child readjusting themselves as they drift back into their little dreamland. and yet, I felt stuck in my own dreamland for those few hours before the rush of life returned to us, and pulled us from our little paradise. the lush plants on your cupboards and shelves cast fascinating silhouettes as the light began to flow in through the window, the ceiling detailing so intricate and beautiful. our feet poked out of the covers at the end of your bed, playing tag with each other, poking and stroking each other's ankles, as if to say:

"I'm still here".

'freezeframe'

Watching the sky turn
every shade of blue
this morning
through your old
terrace window
made me think
of all the sunrises
that I've missed
stuck inside my head
covered up in bed
until almost midday
every other morning

'new perspectives'

What I love so much about kissing
is how it so perfectly adapts to
any romantic situation or circumstance

how it stings or lingers
how it pushes and pulls those
engaged at the lips

intensifying the tension or resolving it
the sudden rush of new beginnings
or the sigh of relief because *finally*

‘you’re kissing’

I wore my favourite lipstick for you today
I thought you'd like to taste it

'santa sangre'

Every time we embrace
you fill in all the negative space
we fill in each other's curves and divots

Late at night in our bed
whenever you aren't here with me
the emptiness feels a thousand times
bigger and heavier
enveloping me in the cold and loneliness
when you are light and warmth

The door that closed behind me
opened the largest window
and through the glass, smiling at
me from the other side, was you.
let me smash the fragile glass
and run into your arms.

Down by the cliffs where the sea meets sandstone and
seaweed scratched and tickled our ankles
we shared a glance that lasted a second too long

in that moment you snatched up my heart like a
helpless fish stranded on the shore
after high tide

'I was the fish, you were the fisherman'

You live next to a bridge
it comforts me to hear
the early morning trains
rushing past as we
snuggle under the sheets
the day has begun
we watch underneath your
window the bustling of cars
people making tracks
bee-lining their way
to office buildings
across the bridge
but we're still here
silent
in our own little haven
nowhere important to be
so let's stay a little longer

I just want to lie with you
under the sheets in your bed.
I just want to observe you as you
come back to life when the sun
starts to peer through your blinds.

I just want to watch you as you
muddle up your face as if you're
scrunching up a piece of paper
and stretch your arms out
as if you're surrendering to God
on Judgement Day.

I just want to see you as your head
turns towards me and your eyes
traverse across the mountainous
contours of the sheets,
the soft curves of my skin,
and meet my gaze.

I just want to be there with you and
smile as we say good morning.

I just want to feel the warmth of
your touch as our legs intertwine,
the electricity coursing through
your bones as our fingers interlock,
the heat from your kiss as your lips
meet my forehead.

I just want every moment,
every single second,
every blink, smile, sneeze.
I just want all of you.

The flutter of eyelashes stops
when our eyes lock
searching each other's souls
for a hint of what they feel

the rush of blood
pulsing through arteries
throbbing in fingertips hanging at your sides
banging drums in ears

observing our bodies' messages
trying to decippher the concealed code of our attraction
a shoulder twisted this direction
feet facing that direction

a glance held a second too long
to remain considered platonic
look away before the blood reaches your cheeks
compromising your visage

heart jerking thuds in your chest
paired with tickling of butterfly wings – just kidding,
those are elephants stomping inside your gut

wind tousling our hair into our eyes
I don't want to be blinded
by the strands of auburn right now
I want to see you

He studies art,
while he himself is art.
his body, his mind,
his soul, his smile is art.
I could study him like a Greek
sculpture, a relief depicting the
wondrous male form.
I could explore every surface,
feel the contours of his muscled
back underneath my fingertips
trace the outlines of his veins
through his skin, study the angle of
his jawline and the hook of his nose.
let my gaze wander over into
his electric blue eyes.

If I could put you on display in an art gallery I would

'you are art'

You're like a library filled
with books that an eager reader
can't wait to open and discover
a story that captures their mind and their soul

A friend once gave me
a tarot reading,
the cards jumped out
of the deck and showed me
our future

'tarot'

I love it when we
wrestle in bed;
my body is wrapped around you,
my knees squeezing your torso,
unrelenting, not letting go.
so you flip me over
onto my back - now I am defenceless.

the delicately laid
white cotton sheets
now a twisted mess,
shoved to one corner of
my queen-sized bed,
the duvet clinging to the edge
before softly toppling off the side.

when we lie into each other
I claw at your back,
your hair falls into my eyes,
the very same ones that gaze into yours.

I love it when you spread your arms out
as I sit on your lap,
you look like a wandering preacher,
caught up in the majesty of the
prophecy playing before your eyes,
the sacredness of intimacy.

The gentlest caress of our bare skin
against our fingertips,
the raw energy pumping through our veins.

unholy are our thoughts,
holy are our bodies as they meet once more.

'preacher'

As we lie there in your bed
and the morning sun glows
through your window
the heavens place a crown
upon your head
a golden halo of sunshine
shimmering over your hair
turning it a warm copper
shade
king of my heart, the skies
bow to you.

When our lips meet
nothing can separate us
we lie there, we stand there
in our own gravity
like a black hole we meet
in the middle and spin in an
intense crush
everything spins with you
even when everything is still and silent
you make me alive

My stomach isn't filled with flutters
or tickled by soft butterfly kisses against the lining,
my stomach is subject to convulsions,
and weightless freefalling.
like a contortionist it bends and squeezes into
uncomfortably tight knots.

The soft swish of
grasses under
the fingertips,
the gentle whooshing
of leaves above our heads.
the chilled breeze
bites at my ankles as
we lie there.
I look across to meet
the electric blue
in your eyes,
the honey in your
auburn mane.
the icy touch
of your fingers
against my thigh
but the warmth of your breath
fogging up in the air.

Was it the sunrise that spanned the edge of the earth at the beach, a sprinkle of hours before we met? or was it the thick amber streetlights that flash at us at crossroads or the traffic cones we passed late at night illuminated by head-lights?

maybe it was the colour of the box of crackers that I bought on the way to the gallery and the sound of their nostalgic crunch? or the tinge of copper in your stubble, or the faded hue of the hot wedges we ate for lunch?

is it the emergency exit sign on my Greyhound bus returning home or my laptop background that drowns my skin in its rich shade? or is it the colour I see behind my eyes as everything else fades into pitch grey?

perhaps it was the sunrise streaming in from your bedroom one morning that washed us in its honey golden glow. or the sunset we watched fall over the city from your living room.

all I know is that this colour never fails to make me think of you.

'orange'

Hold your hand in mine
feel the warmth radiate between us,
the electricity tingling through our fingertips.
let our arms swing like the pendulum
hidden in the belly of a grandfather clock,

feel the security of our fingers intertwined,
like a lock shut tight,
a code a stranger could never decipher,
or like superglue holding us together
before our grasp is torn apart,
and we reach for each other's ghosts through our bedsheets.

hold your hand in mine, tight and unrelenting.
set an imprint deep into my palm,
so once you return to me it fits in place
as if you never left.

I'll never go back to being the same
person I was since you came into
my life

'and it's for the best'

I laugh at the fact that my heart
started beating for you
long before I realised what it meant

I laugh at the fact that
everything between us started with
two awkward thirteen-year-olds
high-fiving instead of hugging goodbye

Imagine
if our love
wasn't like a
forbidden fruit
that we so wish
to take a bite from

if people didn't
look at us with
strange sideward
glances
and meet us
with awkwardness

As I walk
down the
street
listening to
love songs
I realise
it was you
I had been
listening
out for

I remember lying next to you on my towel at the beach, staring at you through the slits between my fingers. I gazed at your brilliant blue eyes, sparkled in the sunlight. your lips looked so soft, so thick and rich, like marshmallows or the few puffy clouds that hovered lazily in the sky. I remember running my fingers through your hair, and how it sent electricty down your spine and through my arm. I remember feeling you wrap your arms around me as we stood in the water; the touch of your hand against my back and my hips. I remember the jolt of thunder in my stomach as I hugged you goodbye, wishing we didn't have to part. I remember the cheek-reddening wave that washed over me as you asked me if I was going to kiss you; and how I never answered you with

my lips.

As we lay there
yesterday
on the grass
as the sun traipsed
across the sky
warming our skin
and the wind brushed
our hair and the
flowers beside us,
it felt as if we were
in our own little
world –
detached from
the passersby
glancing at us
while we ignored them
and instead
kissed frantically –
our own little
movie scene
lying under the
just-summer sun
with a new lover
in a foreign land

I lay on my beach towel, breathing softly as the sun glowed against my bare back. you lay beside me, watching the undulations of my chest. your eyes scanned over me, fingers traversing the soft curves of my hips, and the valley running down along my spine. I turned over and watched you, glancing at your eyes, their astonishing blue. the words you utter leave me speechless, thinking how you could possibly think of me as so beautiful. yet, I bet on the worst of days, you could utter a single word to me and make me feel extraordinary.

'he called me Aphrodite I'

I used to make men into art
and then he spoke those words
and made me into a masterpiece –
a grecian sculpture
spotlighted by the summer sun
come see my skin turn into marble
immortalise my visage and body
in the smooth, cool stone

'he called me Aphrodite II'

When you kissed me
that warm Tuesday afternoon
you awoke and unleashed
something inside me

the wild beast inside
this fragile girl's ribcage
is ready
to come out again

let our mouths press
against each other
in a raging battle
a fight of passion

let our teeth tear
at each other's lips
clawing for more
craving every bite
arms wrap around each other
like twisting vines
obsessed with wrapping us up
begging to come closer

'primal'

My eyes roll back into
the cosmos inside my skull
as your lips travel across
my mouth
your hand crawls up my neck
fingers tightening
sending ten thousand volts
through my spine into my belly
and between my thighs

'day one'

If I had one word to describe you

'unexpected'

If I had every word to describe you

56

'it still wouldn't be enough'

The first word that comes to mind
when I think about you

'magic'

It feels so different
to be wanted
by someone
you didn't even
know existed
a few days ago
and now wanting
to spend every
living breathing
minute looking
into his eyes
begging to see
every piece of him

Just like when we were up
until 5:30am on the first night we met,
I'm up late thinking and writing about you.

'can't get you out of my head'

I don't think that I've
ever met a person who
has changed my life
as quickly and
as much as
you have

'what have you done to me?'

I wish I could relive
that night, when
I shyly pecked you
on the cheek and
ran away like a child –
only for you to pull me
right back in,
and make us lose
ourselves in each other,
as our lips finally met

'first kiss'

Could you please kiss me again?
I think I blinked and missed it.
the pulse of energy as we connected
felt like a flash rushing straight through
my body and out of the tips of my toes.

'wow'

The tattoo of the Norse compass
on your arm led you to me

'Vegvísir'

As we lay there
you asked me to be yours
even after such little time
I couldn't wait to call you mine

'yours/mine'

I never saw you coming
never in my wildest dreams
did I think somebody like
you
could ever come into my life
or fall for somebody like
me

'lucky'

Could you tell when I was terrified
when I told you I loved everything
about you but never just *you?*

could you tell when every little fear
and inhibition that welled up inside
my chest melted away when you
beat me to it?

'I love you'

Hearing three little words that you
never shared with anyone before
makes their meaning all the more
precious to me

'to the moon and back'

The only arguments I hope we ever have are the ones where we fight about who loves whom more.

'I love you more'

Can we just accept that
our love for each other
is so unfathomable
in so many different ways
that we can't put it into words?

'I love you most'

Our love didn't start off as a spark
first, there was nothing
and then there was

'*wildfire*'

Old flames can't hold
a fucking candle
to your bonfire heart

You can hear it in the silence between us
you can see it when we steal glances from each other
you can feel it when you hold and kiss my hand as we walk and drive together

'*you are in love*'

One step inside your house and I already feel welcome.
your bedroom already feels like home.
it feels as if I've known you all my life because your arms
have become the safest refuge I know.

'Coming home'

Alex Bailey Coleman

I love the way you smell
the familiar musk that washes
over my senses as I nuzzle into
your shoulder or snuggle into
your shirt that sits in my closet
or the spritz of cologne that
lingers on my pillowcase

Your voice is like a good whiskey;
smooth and rough and
mellow and smokey and sweet.

'All I want to do is drink it up'

I could drown
in your cologne
and still
die
happy

'suffocate'

A few nights ago,
we watched your favourite
movie together
as we lay there on my bed
blue fairy lights behind us twinkling
watching the camera pan
over the town of Leith, Edinburgh,
I dreamt that we would travel there
together in the future,
and think back to that quiet night
upstairs in my room

'sunshine on leith'

You replaced the teary
spasms in my chest
that sought to drown me
with fits of laughter

you switched out my
anxious heart with one
that skips a beat every time
I see you

'is this happiness?'

I don't want
to ever have to
hide the smile
that spreads
across my face
whenever
you walk through
the door and
light up the room

'joy'

Nothing makes me
smile as much as
seeing you after a
long, hard day

Every night,
in your arms
is where
I long to be

Nobody I know has eyes
quite like yours

'remarkable'

All the small things add up, and
every miniscule thing that I learn
about you I fall even more
in love with.

'details II'

Every day I hear songs that I love and they make me think of you more than I already do

every night I dance in my room like a lovestruck fool and it's all because of you

You fell asleep on my bed tonight. I was in your arms and I couldn't stop
staring at you —
How peaceful you looked. the rhythmic rise and fall of your chest, the ginger
spikes poking through your stubble, the smoothness of your cheeks. I could
feel the contrasted rough and smooth of your forearms lying across your
body and around my waist, and smell the faded scent of your cologne on your
t-shirt, my pillow and my bedsheets.

In the hour that you were resting I could see my life flash before my eyes, real-
ising that all the pain and tears and hurt that I've endured and passed out to
others throughout my life had boiled down to the stillness of this moment. in
the hour that you lay there, so peaceful and quiet, I could see my prayers and
eyelash wishes finally being answered. I could see my future walk out from the
shadows of chaos that stand behind me.

'now all you have to do is stay'

I find there is something
so intimate
about watching you sleep

I find there is something
so intimate
about watching you sleep

The whole world could pass us by,
or crumble in front of our eyes, and
I'd still get lost looking into yours,
kissing your lips and exploring your body.

We might only be human
but the effect you have on me is
otherworldly

The electric shock of your touch
hasn't stopped pulsing through
my system since you first laid
your hand on my skin

Sometimes
there are nights
that I don't
want to rip
your clothes off
and feel our bodies
devour each other
tear and tug and
pull at my hair
or grip my thigh
sometimes
there are nights
that I just want
softness –
to press pause
on the frenzied
anticipation
and instead
to dive into
the tiniest of
details hidden
in the small
of your back
or the rise and fall
of my cheekbones
to be delicate
with our souls
and our fingertips
and with our bodies
simultaneously

The bubbly rush of reassurance and
bliss that my entire body and all
my senses are overcome, as we talk
with each other late at night when
we (read: you) really should be sleeping.

that rush that washes over me like a
weighted blanket being thrown
over me after a long, hard day.
that rush that never fails to come as
words of love and full-bodied promises
escape your lips and meet my ears.

I have a picture of you saved
in my phone that serves as
a reminder of the dreams we share
and hope to fulfill when
the time is right

I pray every day
when I look through
my phone's photo album
that I've dedicated to you
that I never stop smiling
as I swipe to see
the memories we've
collected together

watch the grin spread
across my face
like wildfire
everytime I look down to
see your childish smile
looking back up at me
or as I watch and rewatch
videos of you singing in the car
on the way home

I see us as we drive in your car
as if we were two mysterious lovers
in a movie scene or music video.
life plays to the beat of new songs.

Looking at photos of us,
sitting squashed together in a
themed bar in the first week we
started dating, it makes me think
of how we once spent our existence,
so blissfully unaware of each other.
I pray that we never have to
feign this ignorance again.
to avoid second glances and
awkward "hi's" as we duck our
heads and turn away, strangers
once more.

'please don't disappear'

I see photos that you send me of
yourself and I see the man you are
and the man you will become
all in one.

'my future'

Whilst looking at photos of us
late one night I think about
how we could be showing these
to our own kids one day, and
talking away the days, sharing with
them the stories of how we met and
fell in love.

I don't think I look like
either of my parents,
even you think so when
you look at the pictures –
but you and your brothers
share so many similar features.
you're nearly the spitting image
of your own father
when he was your age.

I think about how I might
look back at snapshots of us
and pick out if our kids have
your nose, or my dimples; maybe
one will have my hazel eyes and
your smile, or share no resemblence
to either or both of us.

I look through the photos I've
saved of you in my phone –
an entire album dedicated to
your body, your face, your smile.
every time I scroll through this
private collection my heart swells
and I wish certain moments could
have lasted forever, frozen in a
place of pure bliss.
tonight as I am swiping between videos
of us chanting Danger Days
in your car, and snapped holding
hands as we walk by the beachside
in the middle of the night, or
smiling with you at a magical bar,
I think to myself

'yes, this is the man I want to marry'

if I were ever to tell you
I don't love or want you

'I'm lying'

I'm terrified that
the promises we make
each other now will
eventually break
I've shared similar sentiments
with other lovers
before you –
and look where they are now!

'my fear'

Is it all right that
I'm terrified
of losing these
feelings
that I have from
every time I
see
hear
talk
to you?
is it okay if
I never want to
move on
from the first
few days of
our love story?
never want to
turn the pages
even if
I want that
too?

You save me from
the doom and darkness
that dwells in my mind.
you hunt down
all the worries that
escape my brain
through my mouth,
trap them inside a mason jar,
place it on the highest shelf
and leave it there.
you protect me from
the numbness and doubts
that creep over and try
to drown me
in my most vulnerable moments,
bringing me back to the surface
with your light and warmth.

The Losing

Nothing is more
soul destroying
than seeing
the man who stood taller
than the trees I climbed
and taught me to be
a superhero
become a shadow of himself
a body no longer
in control of itself
with wandering
empty eyes
and lost words

'grandfather'

This year
God took somebody important from me
but at the same time he led me to you –
somebody who has helped me keep myself together

'I don't believe in Him, but sometimes I do'

Fear is not the monsters
under your bed
or the nightmares
plaguing your dreams
and soulless shadows
lingering in dark corners

fear is the
e m p t y s p a c e s
where you stand
where nobody else
could ever fill the same way

fear is never seeing
the cracks in your smile
so empty,
instead of joyful

fear is hearing
those words
so quiet yet earth-shattering
and hopeless thoughts
linger in the air between us

fear is crying at night
hoping the goodnight
you wished me
isn't the last thing
you will ever say to me

fear is losing the one
who made me strong
and helped me grow
ever stronger still

all the while he was crumbling
around us
a monolith crushed
by the weight and pain
of his own mind

'dad'

Please don't leave me
I'd be so lost without you

I never realised
I was losing you along the way

'losing you'

They say the love between
a father and a daughter
is so strong

why couldn't we find that again?
why did we only
tear at each other with our words?

'hurting the people we love *ourselves*'

Do I ever cross your minds
like a shadow in the mirror
late at night?
do I come knocking at
your locked bedroom doors
or catch your eyes as you drift to sleep?

you tend to visit me
like ghosts beautifully haunting me
with your presence
in the back of my head
and the days of what once was

'ghosts of boyfriends past'

I thought I'd surprise him
after school one day with
his favourite chocolate
because he was at home, sick

I called him on the walk
from the train station and
up the steep road to his house

I told him I was outside,
standing by the letterbox
confused, he asked *why?*
I thought you were in class

I told him I brought chocolate
and wanted to make sure
that he was okay

he told me his sister was home –
a girl I was never introduced to –
and that I couldn't come in

he didn't have to answer the door
because he wouldn't even let me
walk up the driveway

I took the chocolate home instead
and was greeted by my mother
and my grandmother who had
just arrived from the airport

their smiles quickly turned into
looks of confusion and worry
and so I cried into my elbows
and their arms as the evening came

'year 10 romance'

I never met his parents
never got to smile and shake
his father's hand
as I entered his house for the first time
or share stories of high school
with his older sister
who graduated from my school
the year prior
or compliment his mother
on her cooking
when I stayed for dinner
because he never let me stay
and he never let me see or speak to them
he hid us away in the lounge room
with the curtains shut tight
and the door locked
so no unwanted, unknown faces
could see me

'he kept me like a secret'

I remember when we were young
before we became strangers again
I remember when we used to write about each other to each other
I wish I could hear the sweet things
that flowed out of your body and dripped from your lips
one more time

'we were poets'

I wish I had saved some of the
letters I wrote to you
and the ones you wrote for me
so that I could have tapped into
some of the raw emotions
at the source
and remember what it was like
for us to love when we did

'habibi'

I look back at memories
tucked away in the recesses
of my phone
of my computer
of my mind
and I think about how
we thought we knew so much
about everything life had to offer us
when we were still just kids
and we had so much to learn
and so many mistakes to make
before we realised who we really are
and how different we would be
a year later
and how different we are
six years on

'when we were sixteen'

I remember us singing that song
by The Chainsmokers –
the one that never stopped
playing on the radio and the one
I never stopped listening to –
late one night in Wollstonecraft
and how we walked around the
deserted streets together
as a little trio thinking
nothing would change

Saying goodbye to a best friend hurts can more than any break-up could

but when your best friend is the one you break up with, it hurts more than anything else

The addictive, poisonous
essence of sweet sweat and
wanting

I should have seen it in your
eyes but I couldn't meet them —
you only looked at my body

You touched me and turned
me to gold
but when you left I found my
skin tarnished and rusted

Fuck oxytocin,
the stupid chemical
that plays sick jokes
in your brain,
making you believe
something is real

always too good to be true,
because you know that
he'll be gone
when he's finished with you.

You were like nicotine in my veins,
cigarette smoke in my hair and clothes –
you liked to linger long after you left.

you stuck around like gum under my shoe,
my fingernails became dirtied because of you –
black with filth and gunk and muck
that no soap could remove.

you were like a botched tattoo
I got on a drunk night out,
as distorted as my memory, plaguing my mind
and skin with your faded, nightmarish gaze,
but my body soon rejected you.

you were a selfish parasite digging into my body.
time to disinfect the bite.
you were medication that made me worse.
doctor, rewrite my scripts.

you were bad - everybody knew it except you.
but you were so good at it.
your recklessness was an addiction I couldn't kick.

but when you left,

I crashed into a bottomless pit,

craving your destruction again,

ready to crawl back to the depths of habit.

only then did I realise

I wasn't buried. I was flying.

now the high you gave me is well and truly gone.

booted out of my rebooted system.

no more screaming mind

pleading for more of your poison.

no more desperate eyes

searching for the darkness you blinded me with.

I'd rather go cold turkey

for a lifetime than to see

your rotten face again.

'drug'

I just feel so disappointed

in myself for letting me fall
when it was a cliff and not love

in you for letting me think
I could walk on air

Sometimes
it bewilders me
how much
time and energy
I have spent
all in vain
on people who
don't deserve it

Cross my heart
hope you die
because you always
had to lie

cross my heart
hope you cry
when you think
of me at night

cross my heart
hope you freeze
when beg me
on your knees

cross my heart
hope you know
that you'll always
be alone

'poetry for ~~beginners~~ *the broken-hearted'*

Remember every word
you didn't listen to
I remember every word
you left out
I remember every memory
you tossed aside
like rubbish

For weeks I spent feeling utterly unloved as I lay next to him in his bed. every weekend and not a word was uttered between us as we prepared to drift off for the night. just the sound of his staggered breath as he slept, and the staggered sound of my heartbeat in my ears. then the sound of my crawling through the sheets and over his unmoving body and the soft landing of my feet against the carpet as I walked to the bathroom, led by the moonlight. the pathetic shudders of my shoulders and the tremulous breath as my eyes seared and my chest felt crushed and empty. nothing left but withered muscle.

Why did I let myself endure his false love?
why did I pray for his touch
but his presence looked more like a miracle
when his absence put me through hell?

'false god'

It is the colour of our kiss
when you share your bed with me
one fateful night
and the hollowness of my chest cavity
when I no longer want to belong to you

'black'

Our last correspondence
was when you told me
you couldn't wait
to see me again

'so why haven't you?'

Why must I rush things?
the first day I met you
I ruined our friendship
then a week later
it felt like you ruined me

You broke my heart
even though
it never belonged to you
in the first place

The quiet seeds of resentment
sprouted in my chest
and rotted in the earth
on the day you told me
no

that somebody else
crept into your heart
late at night like vines
over old building walls

they're blooming now
in all their glory
showing me the beauty
I would have missed out
on seeing if I had heard a
yes

it seems that while
they may have been
fertilised with
hatred or
jealousy
they were watered with
newfound self-respect
and love

our season may never
have come into full bloom
but sometimes it's better
for weeds to frost over
and rot, so that
better plants may grow.

I cried today
as the plane surged into the sky —
the secret fear of
not making it
hiding deep within my skull —
my deepest fears breaching the
surface that I might not see you
again.

There are some nights when
I can't help but cry myself to sleep
because I can't feel the ghost of
your body between the bedsheets
next to me anymore
I know you'll return tomorrow or
the day after
but the separation sometimes pokes
at the most vulnerable fragments
of my soul

Every person I've ever loved and lost
has never revisited my life.
their ghosts invade my mind occasionally,
haunting me with times near-forgot,
faces once smiling,
now only seen on screens of friends I once knew.
they're all smiling now with people who aren't me.
but I don't blame them,
I have other reasons, too.

I accept the mutual silence
between us.
never to be broken,
never a word, never a crossing of paths at
the same bars or the same places
we used to visit together.

my last ex and I said goodbye at his front gate.
I could tell he didn't want to
walk me back to my car that fateful day.
I like it that way.

but now, I'm scared of the chance that
you might leave, too —
turn your back and change everything
I ever thought about you.

I'm scared of losing the intense passion we share,
only to have intense bitterness take its place –
the same reaction in the pits of me
and my ex's stomachs if perchance we hear
each other's names in everyday conversation.

the threat of losing you clings to my mind,
because I don't want to restrain myself from smiling
if I hear your voice or laugh, because I could
recognise it and remember the first time
it reached my ears.
I'm scared of becoming a shell of who I am
because you aren't here.

'if you ever left'

I want to love you with the same fervour you love me with
but I'm sorry, I'm still learning to love myself
I promise if the time comes
I will return and love you just as much and more

The tears I've shed
for other men
have watered the neglected
gardens of my heart
filling the cracks
where weeds and pretty flowers grow

the tears I shed for you
will drown my ribcage
and flow out through my mouth

'flood my soul'

143

I listen to a song
late one night
to remind myself
of what it felt like
when our love
was young

the nostalgic
hope and warmth
in our hearts
as we sat in your
college dormroom
so many times

rocking
back and forth
to the clap
of the beat
as Jon Bellion
speaks

'two empty chairs'

From all
the pain
they
inflicted
upon me
I picked up
the shards
of my
broken soul
and stabbed
you
with them
as well

'I didn't mean it'

145

When we parted
it felt like
you took
all the joy and
it looked and
felt like
you had taken
all the colours
from my life.

I'm sure that
you would say
the same about me

My fondest memory of us now
is of when we danced in
the middle of the night
on the beach
to a song by my favourite band and
we melted down into nothing more
than two souls
connecting with the
raw majesty of the clashing waves
and the beat of drums and
strums of guitars

'The City by the beach'

147

It was the hope
that I felt when
my aunty told me
about how she found
her "tribe" at uni —
the very same one
I attend now

now I sit in my room
seething, thinking how
I could think that
that was in my cards
in my fate, my future
just like hers

The pain I feel
that I believed them –
telling me that I
always belonged
when they had already
alienated me
long before

149

It won't be tears
that cascade down
my cheek tonight
as I wish myself
to sleep, to erase
the pain and lies.
instead there is
unadultered shame
and bitterness I feel
coursing through my
veins like foggy steam.
shame against myself
for thinking things
would change and
you wouldn't exile
me another time,
and bitterness
against you all for
double-crossing me,
and making me
believe that you
did everything with
the best of intentions,
when it was all lies.

Fool me once
shame on you
fool me twice
it's my fault
for believing you

people have told me
time and time again
that I am one of them
yet I never feel like it
and continue to feel
like an outsider

because we used to share
stories of how we all felt
like sore, sticking-out thumbs
and aliens amongst humans
used by those we once considered
the closest of friends

The disappointment I feel
when I see them all
together again
without me
yet again

'false friends'

The pain is
washed out
by bitterness
and distrust
because
how could
I trust you
when you
already lied
to me once
before?

'false friends II'

I thought you were my tribe
my sisters for life –
but it turns out
you all were just a lesson
I hadn't quite yet learned

'false friends III'

You don't let dead flowers
fill your garden beds,
cut the heads off
and let new life grow
in their place

so why would you
let dead weight fill your heart?
cast out the toxic bodies
and let new life enter
in its place

The Learning

To the little girl who hides in the corner of her room as if it were a fortress protecting her from the hurt and ache outside the fortified walls

to the little girl who dips her head and wraps her arms around her knees like a straightjacket as she locks the doors shut before the tears break them down

to the little girl who isn't little anymore, but feels the same scratching tightness in her throat, sporadic shaking in her chest and ache deep within her hollow belly

It seems that in the most
inopportune moments
my thoughts decide to leave me
nothing but the vast black space
my brain originally occupied

but then in other moments
everything happens at once
everything I want and don't want
to see, hear, think, feel

Frazzled mind like earphones shoved
haphazardly inside my jeans pocket,
wires short-circuiting inside my head.
heartbeat rattling in my ears like a metal jug
clanging agaist a cold tile floor.
I don't know I'm crying.
the tightness in my chest
and the shortness of my breath
the pain at the back of my throat
like walls closing in on themselves.

'stress'

Why do my thoughts sometimes look like highways in peak hour, when every-
thing and everyone is trying to get out all at once?

why do my thoughts sometimes look like an abandoned airport runway,
nobody around to help the stranded passengers?

Sometimes I don't understand
how you could possibly love me
sometimes my mind infects
my heart and makes me feel as if
I'm about to wake up from this dream

Why is it that after so long my brain
continues to work against me, corrupting
my perception of you and our love?

I hate silence but beg for it
stop asking me questions –
I can't stand it
but shower me in attention
until I drown
leave me alone but stay close by
for when I need you
to come back

The other day you could see
the shadows began to surround
me and cloud my brain again
you pulled me out of the
darkening corners of my mind
and showed me the light and
warmth once more

The sick feeling in my stomach
is back
like malevolent moths instead of
sweet, innocent butterflies,
they're gnawing at the lining
rather than giving ticklish kisses

The darkness of my mind looms
around me like a cave
and no light can ever enter.

In my head I hear a sea
crashing against the pale walls
that confine it,
stopping it from pouring out of my eyes,
or overflowing from my ears and nose.

whitewash is catapulted
into the air upon impact,
the splattering against the
trembling waves.

if I look inside myself,
i fear I may drown in
the turmoil, the terror,
the demons of the deep
holding me down, gasping for air,
trapped in their murky lair.

but what if I dive in,
and surrender myself to the tide?
will the heavens part the inky clouds?
settle the frustrated waters?
will everything lie still as it once did,
when life was simpler?

The darkness loomed over me again
like it used to years ago
when people who loved me –
or more accurately, were supposed to –
looked more like hungry vultures
waiting for me to lie down before
they could consume my weak spirit.

'depression I'

Chapped lips and
ripped skin
gnashing teeth and
sore cheeks
the frustrating contrast of
blocked cold nose and
streaming shut eyes
hoarse voice
strained from
back and forth bellowing

I don't often pull out
the small blade hidden
in the depths of my
bedside table
I haven't placed its
sickly sweet edge against
my skin in a long time

friend meets enemy
an old habit
crawling into my life
once again

'shame'

I wish it didn't hurt
or that I bled gold
so then my scars could be
beautiful

I wish my mind wasn't a maze
I can't escape
a puzzle I can't solve

My brain was at war with itself,
its casualties my body and my soul;
shellshocked from the all-
consuming nightmares that plagued
both my days and my nights,
wishing for dreams of warmth to
greet and comfort me again

'depression II'

I cried myself to sleep for the
first time in a long while.
watching social media posts for
hours upon hours of my friends
at a party I wasn't invited to.
seeing them tag each other in posts
they know I'd enjoy, too, but
always forgetting my name.
hearing of their wonderful times
together grabbing coffees before
class, never thinking to see if I have
class that day too, the way
we used to.

It's finally come back up.
That feeling of never being enough,
feeling as if I will never truly find
myself a lifelong group to belong
to.
The feeling of having things
planned behind my back, talking
about me like an outsider –
a complete and total stranger.
then smiling those fake smiles and
being nice to me as if I don't have
a clue.

Surrounded by people
who I think
I get along with,
but always feeling
like a stranger
in a crowd of
close friends.

Feeling so lost that no expression of
closeness and familiarity can make
you feel special or part of a group.

I look around at the detritus of my life,
crying and terrified of the wreckage;
all the friendships and loves looking for
the witch that cursed me.
I find myself staring at the magic mirror
and the cracked glass, finally seeing myself
in my true, gruesome form

'I am the villain in my own fairytale I'

I am the girl who cried wolf when it was
me, with bloody claws and reddened fangs,
now emerging from the cave in tatters,
no longer fur-coated and blood-thirsty,
completely unaware of the pain I inflict
upon a wicked and cruel night.

'I am the villain in my own fairytale II'

My heart now feels
the familiar ache of
nothingness once more,
my wrists begging to feel
the metallic sting of
living and dying
at the same time
once more,
and again
and again.

'depression III'

There is something wonderfully morbid in watching
the blood mix with the warm water as it flows and
bubbles down the drain of my shower late at night.

it reminds me of that disturbing, yet oddly mesmerising
sensation that overcomes you when you see or feel
a broken bone; the limb or joint not quite how it should be.

'morbidity'

sometimes I think it's okay
to feel a little numb
it reminds you to be thankful
for the days when you feel
the colour of the sun
against your skin,
the electricity that pulses
through your bloodstream
when you genuinely smile
and when it feels as if
you're seeing everything up close
for the first time all over again.

'feeling'

My heart,

so hesitant to let another reach into its depths and see the damage,

still wavers from time to time when you promise to never grimace at the scars.

When you are strong for me
you make me stronger
when the time comes that
you fall down
I will be strong for you

The Living

183

Take my hand as
our journey begins –
will you wander with me?

‘I am a wanderess’

Come on an adventure
with me
we'll whisper innocent
phrases into each other's ears
while we dream of
sinful deeds

Don't point at the map
don't show me your dream holiday destination
and don't tell me where you want to visit.
show me with your eyes
how the names of unknown and faraway places
dance across the traffic signs
point out to the highway
search the horizon as it transforms every mile.
search inside yourself and
let your soul guide you across this land.

'where to next'

The relentless sleepless nights of wanting to write
but ending up with
nothing

then the instant onslaught
of every idea rising up to the surface like a
breaching humpback
between the heads of a rocky coastline
now my head is filled and overflowing with ideas
my lips dripping with undiscovered phrases

the cool force of my bedroom fan
the gentle icy glow of streetlights outside my house
what time is it?
who cares – I need to write.

The curve in my back is
starting to ache
as it so often does
when I curl over my laptop tonight –
my posture has deteriorated
like the walls of
an abandoned cottage
in a nice suburb

it's always like this –
the intense rush
the sudden need to write
just to spill every syllable
every letter
every thought and dream
out onto the page
a splash, the splatter
against a literary canvas

The insatiable desire
to write everything
that pops into
my head is back

but nothing
is rushing through it
only white noise playing
in my grey matter

and songs
scrambled together
like radio static

why is it always like this?
it's the middle of the night and
he's asleep and
I need sleep.

but my brain won't
seem to switch off
my heart feels like
I'm running out of time

'the right/write time'

189

There are more things
that I wish to tell you
I hope to say these
sweet things every day
as we grow old together

When I look at you
a million things that
I could tell you
bubble under the surface,
deep within my heart

I hate how although
there are more things that
I want to tell you than
there are stars in the sky
I can't manage to find the right ones

Darling there are so many things
I wish to say and tell you
but I don't have the words

The jacaranda trees paint the world
the most beautiful shade of purple
that I've ever seen.
the gardenias' aroma dances up my
nose and is carried through the air
by the wind.
Christmas is right around the
corner and everything feels right,
so sure about itself.
all because of you,
everything is better.

The sun finally decided
to peer out
of the clouds after the thunderstorm

The sun feels warmer against
my skin this morning
the wind doesn't dig in its icy
teeth or scratch against my
face with its chilled claws
the weight on my shoulders
has been lifted by the
butterflies fluttering through
my system
the glow from your skin has lit
me up inside
and out

Above my head one day
the sky is painted
with lines of white
one after another

piece them together to form
letters
words
names

it reminds me to
stop
more often and look
up

'clouds'

Do you ever wonder if the stars
look up at us, too?

You touch the hearts of others
and broaden their minds
they first only see the sunrise but
after you they see the entire horizon

Words can only hurt
if you allow them
to possess more power
than you allow yourself

Men, watch your
filthy fucking mouths

'catcalling'

The fear of thinking it is
is often far greater than
that of knowing it is

'thinking/knowing'

The fear of thinking it is
is often far greater than
that of knowing it is

I know I die in my dreams
when my vision goes white
and I wake up in tears
I can often still feel the pain
in my chest as I try to drift back off

'nightmares'

I wish for long nights that feel like lucid dreams

202

Give me back the 5am trainings
and the sunrises that coloured
my dull existence and made my day

Greeted by the sunrise
and the warmth of true peers
oars in the water
quelling all fears

tied to school
but a lifestyle at large
for the demand placed on oneself
makes the mind and body hard

but at the heart of the endeavour
which remains long after the last stroke ends
in the camaraderie having done it
with great friends

'rowing'

She watches the asphalt beneath
the bus tyres rush past the bottom
of the window in a slate grey blur
tufts of grass growing on
the edge of the highway
are reduced to impressionistic
swishes ingrained into her memory

the clouds overhead dapple
themselves across the sky's expanse
allowing the desperate sun
to glisten through briefly

two small white cars and a grey one
coated in dust make an appearance
only to be swallowed by the seats
in front of her

she notices the headache swelling
in the front of her mind –
a certain heaviness in her abdomen
reminding her of the classic
sickness symptoms she would get
as a child

the last time she was unwell was in
Tasmania six years prior
when her father recklessly carried
her family around the roads that
traced the curves and contours of
the southern mountains

she had been looking down at her
phone and listening to rainforest
noises when she should have been
appreciating the countryside meta-
morphosing outside

the winding of valleys
undulating of hills
the shades of green clustering into
one lush heap around her
the freckling of sunlight against
her face and her forearms
as she types up notes for later

the rushing of wind and water
sounds from her earphones washes
away the guttural humming of the
engine and the clattering of the shell
of the bus as it bounces over
uneven pavement

she notices the all-too-familiar
windmills turning like giant totems
dancing for the wind gods further
ahead to her left
she'd be arriving soon
so, naturally, a nap would be nice

'un-natural ambiences'

The point of the Telstra tower in the
distance, a strange, concrete
iconoclast, standing tall and
proudly, casting its shadow across
Lake Burley-Griffin.

the university doesn't sit in the
darkness – I know because the
sunlight pours in and over me,
heating your room like a sauna.

being so close to everything.
I remember the red gravel outside
the war memorial, and the dust that
gathers in your throat as you run across it,
and the flag flapping in the wind
above the top of the memorial.

As the sun sets over
the glistening modern
buildings and the trees
cast their dappled shadows
over us, we walk through
the lush campus park

I can't help but gaze
at your face, looking forward.
You tell me to watch the road,
as if it shows me my future.

I reply:
I don't need to
when I can look at you.

I saw a mother at the airport
I saw her smile, the lovely creases
weaving their way across her face,
such delicate contours, so telling of
a life well-lived.

I saw her son at the gate
I saw his smile, wide and joyful, his
grin, plush skin, face graced with
gorgeous youth and innocence.

I saw her husband
I saw his eyes, aged by the sun and
years of memories flashing before
his irises.

I saw how he looked at her,
at their son. the three of them together.
in that singular moment, just a flash of existence.

In this seemingly regular reunion
I saw their past, present and future
all at once, as the son leaped into
his mother's outstretched,
welcoming arms

I saw the husband greet his wife
with a small kiss that translated to
more than a thousand I love you's.
I saw them walk together, hand in
hand in hand, out of the gate and
towards home.

'I saw more than just a family'

The lights of a city,
a myriad of electronic signs and advertisements,
traffic lights, headlights, streetlights, house lights,
the glow of smartphones in the dim haze of twilight.
I look across the vast city, a
wash of pinks and yellows
settles over the edge of the horizon.

'coming into sydney'

I love that my mother wishes
for me to travel more
to dance across borders
without a care

I love that she wishes
for me to be happy
to know what it feels like to
glow from within

I love that she wishes
for me to be healthy and
to never fear that my body might
one day fail me

I love it when my mother wishes
many things for me
except when she wishes that
I continue to find love
in people I've yet to meet and
futures I've yet to take part in

I hate when she wishes me
these things
when I have already found them
in you

'wishes'

I enjoy the tranquillity
of the morning, the
quite drone of cars
in streets passing by
with the callous squawk
of cockatoos
I like the hazy glow
of low-hanging clouds
meeting the rising
sun, peering over the
shadowy trees and
long powerlines

'waiting for the 7:33 bus'

We are like nomads,
hopping between locations like chess pieces,
moving between the purposes we find and
the ones we continue to seek out.

'nomads'

I like to walk around late at night
in the middle of my street
as everyone else is
silent and sleeping.

I like to watch my footprints
appear against the damp asphalt
and my breath fogging up in the crisp air.

I like to watch my shadow
warp and fade as I walk
under the streetlights.

Wandering down my street
seeing everything familiar look different in the dim light
watching as my shadow skews and stretches as the lights move overhead
hearing the rain start to patter down on the cars and roofs
feel the drops' gentle kisses against my hot and tired skin and
trickle onto my scalp through my sunbleached hair
stopping in the middle of the road to look up at the patchy clouds and inky
sky

'night rain'

I walk down
unknown streets
to find pieces
of myself
late at night
watching the
streetlights
above me like
a halo in the sky
waiting for it
to wash me
of my sins and
insecurities

Walking around with you at 2:30am
when everything else falls quiet and
everyone is asleep, is the time when
I feel most alive

I knew I would be way too
powerful if my brain worked the
way it is scientifically assumed to

'neurodivergent'

I am not a woman
I'm a goddess

I am not a woman
I'm a gender non-conforming deity

I am not a woman
I'm a brain controlling a meat-suit around this earth

I am not a woman
I'm a conscious being who is self-conscious

I am not a woman
I'm the songs I listen to,
the books I read, the films I watch and
the people I meet

I am not a woman
I'm feeling too much and too little at the same time

I am not a woman
I'm attachment issues and
commitment issues at the
same fucking time

I am not a woman
I'm terrible at falling asleep
and worse at waking up early

I am not a woman
I'm a disappointment sometimes,
a joy rarely and an annoyance often

I am not a woman
I'm too loud when I speak my mind

I am not a woman
I'm shamed too much about
too many things

I am not a woman
I'm a fucking mess

I am not a woman
I'm a walking contradiction
that changes her mind and
can never make it up

I am not a woman
I'm a person looking for purpose
in life

I am not a woman
I'm more than what that purpose
gives me

I am not a woman
I'm more than what people
think I am

I am not a woman
I'm exactly what I want to be

'existential crises'

I stood outside and
bathed in the rays of the
almost full moon tonight and
became more of myself again

washing away the past,
the monotone and dull grayscale
of what our lives have become
once more.

'as lockdown sinks in'

I thoroughly dislike the dizzying
dull feeling of having all the joy
and energy sucked out through my
skin after any outing I have
nowadays.
now that we can see our friends
again, after the fact, I feel like a sad
balloon, helium leaking from
within, eventually drooping out of
the air and onto the floor after a
party.

'as lockdown lifts'

I missed the rush of
adrenaline through my
veins that feels like
race-cars speeding
along their track
when I complete
a new course,
the familiar clap
of my palms against
my friends' as I
walk back to them
after watching me
grapple with my fears

'bouldering'

I sometimes am overcome with
the undeniable urge to sit
in the waves and let them
wash over me so I don't have to
feel my tears
on my dry cheeks

Let the water wash over you
cleanse your sins
the inky night sky cast over us
its infinite majesty

When I saw my hair
in the mirror
for the first time
I felt tears
well up inside me
for I saw a girl whom
I had abandoned
a side of me
I had lost
many moons ago
oh, how I wished
to meet her again
for so long,
to reconnect with the soul
I once was.

'the day I found myself again'

When my head feels like
it's being cracked open under
the foot of a goliath barbarian
your smile and love are the ingredients
of the magic spell that revives me

'my special spellcaster'

I would march through the lair of Tiamat for you
slay a Death Tyrant and ride a centaur into battle and
across the Material Plane for you

'dungeons and devotion'

Fairy lights awaken something childish in me,
transport me back to cheeky times
of laugher and magic,
flashing green, blue, red, yellow,
staring into their soft rainbow glow
until my vision blurs.

Behind every fairytale
sat the lonely damsel, who
thought she was(n't) good enough

It was when
I came
to the shore
late that night
and walked
jeans first
into the sea
that I
became
a mermaid
again

You better watch out,
this princess just became a motherfucking queen

'an ode to Amanda Lovelace I'

This little mermaid is going to write her own happy ending, thank you very much.

'The End –
an ode to Amanda Lovelace II'

237

I've had so many loves
in my short life
they all began the same
soaring free and high
above the heavens and cloud nine
for a brief yet sublime moment
whilst I waited patiently
and expectantly
for them to eventually
crash back down to earth
many of my friends
will look at me and
they will see me as
the one who is never
single for very long
and maybe they are right
I've had so many words

trapped inside my head

unwilling to take flight

from my quivering lips

but later when all is left

unsaid but done

they will eventually

escape through either

the tips of my aching fingers

or a neglected pen onto paper

so many feelings and

unspoken broken promises

and things hide deep

inside my soul

never to be shared with the

faceless, nameless people

in my stories

and so I write

'I love therefore I write'